THE HIGH ROAD STREATHAM
AN ARCHITECTURAL APPRECIATION
by
Graham Gower

The Streatham Society

First published in 2008 for
The Streatham Society
219 Sternhold Avenue
Streatham
London SW2 4PG
by
Local History Publications
316 Green Lane
Streatham
London SW16 3AS

Copyright © Text Graham Gower 2008
Copyright © Layout & illustrations: Local History Publications 2008

All rights reserved. No part of this publication may be reproduced, stored in a retrieval system, or transmitted, in any form, or by any means, electronic, mechanical, photocopying, recording or otherwise, without the prior permission of the publisher and the copyright holders.

ISBN 978 1 873520 70 3

THE HIGH ROAD STREATHAM

Bank Parade, Streatham Common (see No. 109)

INTRODUCTION

The High Road Streatham - An Architectural Appreciation

Streatham High Road is one of the ancient highways of London. Its origins are Roman, dating to the 1st century AD. Until the 19th century the High Road, along with the nearby Roman road of Stane Street (A24 Balham/Tooting Road), were the main thoroughfares leading south out of London. Throughout history, Streatham High Road has been known by various names. Being a major roadway, it was commonly known as the King's, or Queen's, highway although certain sections had their local names. The stretch from approximately Gracefield Gardens to Streatham Place was anciently known as Burstow or Bristow Causeway. As the road passed through Streatham and Leigham village, it was known as Stretham Street. The designation of Streatham High Road and Streatham Hill came with suburban development.

Along Streatham High Road history has moved. Roman merchants, Saxon settlers, Viking raiders, Medieval armies, Royal retinues and ordinary people have made their way along what is now one of the busiest routes in London. The High Road we see today is a far cry from what it was like prior to suburban development, which began in earnest from the mid-1870s. Before this time, the highway ran through a mixed landscape of woodland, cultivated fields, parkland and private estates. By the 1900s the High Road through Streatham had changed beyond recognition, particularly that of central Streatham. Stretching from the border with Croydon at Norbury, residential and commercial properties flanked the road all the way into London.

The process of suburbanisation introduced our first local townscape. This focused on

418-420 Streatham High Road (see No. 106)

3

central Streatham and endowed the area with some notable Victorian properties. To the north and south of Central Streatham, large mid - to late-19th century houses, set back behind decorative gardens, dominated the road. In these areas, later developments took place as Streatham moved into the 1920s and 1930s. This period saw the last of many phases that were to shape the present townscape of Streatham and to give the High Road its particular architectural look, notably at Streatham Hill after road widening which occurred during the mid 1920s.

However, the High Road is a creature of change, as commercial and social tastes move on. Here and there modern buildings have been injected into the traditional townscape, many shop fronts have been changed and architectural additions made, which all add visual texture. As I write, new plans are afoot which will see some radical changes to the environment of our High Road as the new century unfolds. New building will appear, reflecting social change and current tastes in architecture and design. Other buildings, familiar to generations of Streatham people will, unfortunately, disappear into history. This is part of the slow evolution of our High Road, which began as a scattering of cottage shops and road side services to evolve into the road we see and use today.

The importance of the architectural heritage of the High Road warranted the creation of the Streatham High Road and Streatham Hill Conservation area by Lambeth Borough Council in 1999. This encompasses the buildings stretching from Telford Avenue to the United Reform Church at Streatham Common, but excludes the Leigham Court Estate (ABCD Estate) at Streatham Hill. This residential development is protected under another Conservation order.

This is a general architectural guide to the rich and varied architecture to be seen along the High Road. A close look at the architectural detail and style of the buildings will be rewarding. Look, for example, at the brickwork, window surrounds, doors, roof designs, stonework, entrances, rainwater heads, chimney stacks etc. - there is much to find and see. Perhaps you may agree, or disagree, with my comments on the buildings, once you have looked at them yourself. Nevertheless, enjoy them and whenever possible view them from the opposite side of the road, where a better appreciation will often be found. The architecture of our High Road is unique, especially the buildings of the 1920s and 1930s, which are not seen in such concentration outside central London. In addition, the Victorian and Edwardian aspect of the High Road offers good architecture, enhancing the visual quality of our townscape. When you undertake this walk, remember it is one of the longest commercial and shopping High Roads in Europe – some 2.5 km. The walk starts at Streatham Place/Chistchurch Road and finishes at the Norbury boundary at Hermitage Bridge.

Graham Gower

St. Leonard's Church (see No. 88)

Streatleigh Court (see No. 12)

Streatham High Road - East Side.

1. 5-9 STREATHAM HILL.

Two large detached mid-Victorian houses, Nos. 5, 7 & 9, last of their type to survive along the High Road, except for two near Streatham Common. Standard period design with stepped entrance flanked by Ionic columns; however, both houses have been modernised with the loss of some original features. Note the architraves around the windows, particularly on No. 7, and the additions of dormer windows to No. 9.

2. CLAREMONT ESTATE.

Adjacent is the Claremont Estate, dating to the mid-1960s. The design is straightforward with minimal decoration and the plainness is relieved by the balconies and alternating areas of yellow brick and white rendering. Note the corrugated iron fronts to the balconies. Comprises of six blocks overlooking green areas.

3. PULLMAN COURT.

A building of style. A pioneering piece of architecture, deriving from the ideas of the international modernist movement of the 1930s,

5-7 Streatham Hill

Pullman Court

Claremont Estate (East)

notably the Bauhaus style from Germany. One of the few early examples of this style of architecture in the country. Designed by Frederick Gibberd in 1935. Grade II* listed. Built with the latest amenities, such as roof terraces, a swimming pool, restaurant, landscaped grounds and lock-up garages. The flats, 218 of them, were well equipped with the latest mod-cons and stylish furniture designed by Gibberd. The most impressive part of the Court are the blocks fronting the High Road, with their geometric look and glazed stair wells projecting out and above the blocks like towers. The rear block has seven storeys while the side blocks, which flank the main driveway, are five storeys. Note the modernistic use of metalwork, particularly along the roofline and the projecting balconies. Architecturally, one of the most important 20th century buildings in London. Originally, the development was to be called Relay House. Was built on the site of the Royal Asylum of St. Anne's Society, an imposing classical styled building erected in 1826. Best viewed from Tierney Road, opposite.

Bus Garage opposite Telford Avenue

4. TELFORD AVENUE BUS GARAGE.

Originally built in 1891-92 as a tram depot for the Brixton Hill – Kennington cable car tramway. In 1904, the route was converted to electricity. The depot was enlarged in 1904-06 and in 1911. Closed in 1951. During 1950-53, the present bus garage was built. Plain and functional looking building with minimal decoration, save for tile cladding to relieve the bare brickwork. The frontage has a small walled green area with seats to add some visual effect. Architects Adie Button and Partners.

BEGINNING OF THE CONSERVATION AREA (CA54) From Wavertree Road to Hopton Road.

5. CORNER FIELDE.

Situated on the corner of Wavertree Road, previously the site of Streatham Hill College, Corner Fielde dominantly stands as a regular block of 1930s residential architecture, with brickwork giving some decoration in band and raised forms. The design of the apartment block was by Toms and Partners and received its first tenants in 1937. At the time of building, Corner Fielde was advertised as being Mayfair in Streatham, with spacious and luxurious accommodation, tiled kitchens with refrigerators, central heating, constant softened hot water and electric lifts. Note the art-deco styled entrance framed with chunky looking pillars, the door design and the brass plate to one side with 'Broadway' style of lettering. Also, the decorative frieze between 3rd and 4th floors. View the side elevation in Wavertree Road and the side entrance.

6. WAVERTREE COURT.

Built upon the site of two early Victorian properties, the Court looks Dutch in style, and is distinctive with its rendered and white painted exterior and dormer windows set into the mansard roof. Wavertree Court was built in 1933 some years earlier than Corner Fielde, to the designs of Frank Harrington. With the development came landscaped gardens set out between the blocks of flats, which can be viewed from Wavertree Road. Note the decorative brick wall and the use of stone for effect and original name sign on corner.

7. 39-43 STREATHAM HILL

Following from Wavertree Court is a sequence of properties, notably the small, inserted house, No. 39, attributed to the 1930s and imparting a Mediterranean flavour. Note the decorative iron work over the window. Next is a plain single story building rendered in white which adjoins a modern construction, Streatham Hill Primary Health Centre. This is a plain functional building, built during the early 2000s, the main feature being the central tower with its large glazed stair well and entrance area. The rest of the frontage is stonework broken by large window areas. Next is a vacant plot awaiting development.

Corner Fielde

Wavertree Court

8. WYATT PARK ROAD TO THE LEIGHAM COURT ESTATE (THE ABCD ESTATE).

On the corner of Wyatt Park Road, No. 45, is a post second world war building erected on a bomb site about 1955. A plain building of brick and stone, with stonework being used to create a visual effect, as seen on the corner end with its tower like style. Some minor styling around the first floor windows, brick patterning below the parapet and an attractive period balcony with iron railings adds interest. Note the dormer windows. The building was extended on the right side during the early 1960s.

Adjoining this building is a recent construction in the contemporary style built in 2006 on the site of the Lex Brookland Garage complex and includes Wheatley Court. A plain building which blends architecturally with the following sequence. Some use of colour enhances the frontage. Note the covered balcony on the top floor, the use of stone stringing and the arch design, which gently leads the eye to the next building. Next is the first block of the ABCD estate. On the wall, by the side entrance, is a property boundary stone of the Artisans', Labourers', & General Dwellings' Company.

9. LEIGHAM COURT ESTATE.

Also known as the ABCD Estate after the principle roads in the development. Stretches from Downton Avenue to Amesbury Avenue. This estate is not included in the Streatham High Road and Streatham Hill Conservation Area, being a separate Conservation Area (CA31) created in 1981. Built by the Artisans', Labourers', & General Dwellings' Company from 1894 to 1905 with later developments finishing by 1928. The designers were Rowland Plumbe and Harry Bell Measures. Named after an 18th century country house and grounds previously sited here. The architecture of the estate is visually very busy, particularly along the High Road frontages. Much use is made of red, yellow and glazed bricks, terracotta work and tiles for effective decoration. Note the finely made swag, alive with detail, and the graceful swan neck feature above the entrance to No. 61. Observe the various shaped gables with attendant decorative features, the corner buildings with their rounded or angled mini 'steeples', the attractive looking oriel windows on the corner of Cricklade Avenue. Note also the grand looking entrances and the different styles of window, including the dormer windows. Although the styles are very mixed, there is continuity in the design, brought about by yellow brick coursing and a continuing cornice. Adjoining the estate and leading round into Leigham Court Road is a parade of lock up shops built about the 1920s.

Shops fronting Streatham Hill on the Leigham Court Estate

THE HIGH ROAD STREATHAM

South London Press Building

10. SOUTH LONDON PRESS BUILDING, 2-4 LEIGHAM COURT ROAD.

An imposing building, which along with Streatleigh Court, dominates the High Road end of Leigham Court Road. The South London Press building, which stands behind Streatleigh Court, was built in 1935. An addition was made to the building in 1963. The architecture of this building is geometrical, relying on horizontal and vertical lines for visual effect. The predominant feature is the central tower, a feature incorporated into the brick built façade and breaking the monotony of the horizontal window line. The stylistic clock, which was a feature of the tower, has been removed in recent years.

11. DORCHESTER COURT, DORCHESTER PARADE, LEIGHAM COURT ROAD.

The first introduction to this small residential development is Dorchester Parade, which butts against the South London Press building, further along Leigham Court Road. It is readily recognisable by its attractive 'Tudorbethan' half timbered frontage which faces Leigham Court Road. Note the quaint restaurant which retains much of its originality. Next to this is Dorchester Court, which sits back almost unnoticed from Leigham Court Road. This residential development relies on brickwork and white painted rendering set under a green glazed pantile roof for its visual effect. The development dates to 1935 and is attributed to the architect H. W. Binns.

12. STREATLEIGH COURT.

Standing on the corner of Leigham Court Road, this lofty and imposing block of flats dominates this part of the High Road. Its style is simple with

Streatleigh Court

some decorative brickwork set beneath the angled bay windows. The main feature of this block are the four 'eyebrow' styled balconies, each likened to the bridge of an ocean going liner, which decorate the north corner of the building. This typically 1930s block was designed in 1937 by Harrington's the architects, replacing an early Victorian mansion called Streatleigh Court. The block sets the architectural style of the High Road on approach to central Streatham (see picture page 4).

13. THE PICTURE HOUSE (PREVIOUSLY THE REGAL/ABC CINEMA).

Recently converted into residential flats. The cinema was one of the last pre-war buildings to arise along the High Road. When built as the Regal Cinema in 1938, it was in the forefront of modern design, with its use of large faience tiles of black and cream decorating a streamlined façade and an Art Deco side tower. The design is by William Reddell Glen and, being a building of architectural interest and importance, was listed Grade II in 1998. In later years, it became the ABC Cinema. During 2007 the auditorium and stage of the cinema were knocked down and replaced with residential flats, while the front façade and foyer, with its period interior, has been retained with minimum alterations. Some modern Art Deco styling can be seen in the design of the flats. Note the bold balconies seen to the side. Next to the cinema is the old Genevieve Public House, recently called the Baroque, now the Mint restaurant. The public house opened in 1967 and was built upon an open space next to the cinema, previously used as a car park. It was designed by Collins Ltd for ABC Cinemas and offers little architectural merit.

The Picture House

THE HIGH ROAD STREATHAM

Norwich House

14. NORWICH HOUSE, 9-11 STREATHAM HIGH ROAD.

A little out of keeping with the adjoining architecture, Norwich House, Nos. 9-11, is nevertheless an interesting building. It was built around 1964 and is typical of the architecture arising at this time. The building, designed by Scott Brownrigg and Turner, replaced the last surviving Victorian mansion standing along this stretch of the highway. Utilising the narrow High Road frontage the building sits at right angles to the road, with the end elevation being the front. This frontage looks like an inverted 'T' with a blank looking central tower block, enlivened by single storey appendages with shops. Being typical of the period, it is finished using roughcast prefabricated concrete panels. The main part of the six storey building can be seen at the rear, where the architecture is visually a little more interesting. Behind is Cromer Court.

15. CATON MANSIONS.

Adjoining is Caton Mansions, a name taken from a Victorian mansion which previously occupied the site. This two storey apartment block with shops was built about 1940, and seemingly the last of the pre-war buildings in Streatham. The main features are the bay windows and a central panel below the stepped parapet. Little further decoration of note. Behind the building is Chalcot

Caton Mansions

Mews, a small residential development built during the 1980s, and accessed by a square archway carrying the name.

16. LEIGHAM HALL.

Taking its name from the old medieval manor of Leigham, Leigham Hall Mansions is another of the pre-war residential blocks that give much of Streatham High Road its 1930s look. Built around 1936 the blocks of Leigham Hall were designed by R. Toms and Partners for the Bell Property Trust, and at the time of building were advertised for their luxurious amenities, such as constant hot water, tiled bathrooms and electric lifts. There was also a swimming pool for residents. Designed with many features in the Art-Deco style, Leigham Hall is indeed a building of its period. Observe the stylistic entrance doors with French influenced ironwork with leaping gazelles, iron work on the above balconies, and the glazed arched stairwell above. Also, the green glazed pantile roof, popular during the 1930s, which runs the length of the frontage above the shops.

Stonework brightens the end corner. Not to miss is the 1930s enamel Streatham High Road street sign above the last shop before Leigham Avenue.

Leigham Hall Parade

Streatham Court

17. STREATHAM COURT.

A large group of flats set back from the High Road and behind Leigham Hall. Built around a formal garden area. The blocks are approached from the High Road through a grand looking 'neo-classical' stone archway. Designed for the Bell Property trust by R.Toms and occupied from 1936. Like the other Bell High Road developments, Streatham Court was advertised as being a delightful example of skilful planning and situated in the most favoured part of Streatham. Again, there are typical 1930s design features to be seen and appreciated, particularly the decorative copper panels set above the entrance doors and in the general look of the development. Note the green pantile roof line, same as Leigham Hall.

18. LEIGHAM AVENUE.

Originally, the trackway to Mount Nod Farm, Leigham Avenue was originally developed during the early 19th century. At present, it has a mixed development with many architectural styles to be seen. Observe some remaining shop fronts, albeit much changed in recent years, built for Leigham Hall and the High. Notably there is Manor Court, three blocks built around a landscape garden area and designed by Toms and Partners for Bell Properties. When completed by 1938, the Court was advertised as being 'The most economical Luxury Flats in the district' and boasted of having central heating, constant hot water, uniformed porters and attractive gardens. Other amenities included a swimming pool, bowling green and a pavilion for dancing. The look of the building is Dutch in style and relies on white painted brickwork, mansard roofs and Art Deco entrances for general effect. Endsleigh Mansions is a three story block of flats, brick built with tiled bays and attributed to the architect John. S. Quilter. Built during the mid-1930s. Basic in style and retaining many original features, such as the Art Deco styled leaded lights, which emphasise the stair wells, and the signage boards. The three blocks making the mansion enclose a garden area. Note the original outside wall.

19. THE HIGH

The most impressive array of flats along the whole length of the High Road – the largest of the interwar developments. Built as five large protruding blocks connected to a continuous block at the rear and with High Road shops beneath a glass canopied walkway, The High received its first residents in 1937. This was another architectural adventure by R. Toms and Partners for the Bell Property estates and was

The High

advertised as being 'Luxuriously appointed' and a building of 'imposing design'. The overall decoration is restrained, relying on brickwork for effect. This is particularly noticeable at the angled end of the block at Leigham Avenue, where relief brickwork gives the impression of square columns. These are finished with stone tops and bases. Note here also the bay window with decorated metal panels, which highlight this corner. A projected cornice links the blocks. Also observe the plain brick balustrade above the shops and the mix of rounded and squared bay windows of the central rear block. Note the entrances with their decorative ironwork and the bold sign 'The High' above the arch. To the rear of the building are the garages and swimming pool, features that were a selling point at the time of building. The original canopy over the pavement, a particular feature of this development, has been replaced.

20. ELGAR HOUSE.

Standing in some contrast to The High, Elgar House was built on a derelict site awaiting development before the second world war intervened. Not imparting any distinctive style Elgar House is nevertheless typical of its time. Designed by William Clark in 1960 it relies on bands of windows and panels running horizontal across the front elevation for its visual effect - grid like. The angled entrance is set aside in Gracefield Gardens and adjoining is Raeburn Court, a red brick residential block of five floors built at the same time. Beneath the block is a Kwik Fit garage, and to be seen in the forecourt by the pavement is the last surviving mile stone from Streatham High Road. The stone, with the wording 'Royal Exchange 6 miles', was removed from a position just to the north from outside the old Pump House, and dates to the 18th century and the days of the Turnpike Road.

Elgar House

21. ASTORIA MANSIONS AND PARADE.

A plain looking residential and commercial development dating to 1933. However, there is some decorative brickwork which breaks the formality of the building which over the years has lost many of its stylistic shops fronts, notably the high Art Deco styled County of London Electricity Supply showrooms (later LEB) on the corner with Gracefield Gardens. To the rear are garages and steps to a terrace which give access to the flats above the shops. Note the original name sign on the side of building.

22. ODEON CINEMA.

A grand looking building sitting well back from the High Road and presenting a mixture of architectural styles much favoured by the architects of the interwar years. The Streatham Astoria opened to the public with great ceremony on Monday June 30th 1930 at 7.30 p.m. The designs of this foray into architectural fantasy came from the notable architect Edward. A. Stone, who was responsible for many iconic cinema designs in London. In keeping with company policy, the Astoria was designed as an 'Atmospheric Theatre' with an interior style

Astoria Mansions and Parade

extravagantly centred on the ancient Egyptian style, with the auditorium colour scheme being predominantly red, gold and green and highlighted by concealed lighting. A magazine of 1930 describes a room in the upper foyer being decorated with an 'Egyptian female figure bathing in a lotus-filled pool above a settee, which in turn has a glass panel at its base to give the effects of rippling water.' In the pre-war years, live entertainment complimented the showing of feature films and many famous dance bands played there as part of the entertainment. In 1939, the Astoria Chain of cinemas was sold to Oscar Deutsch (ODEON - Oscar Deutsch Entertains Our Nation), and in 1941 was acquired by the Rank organisation. Later modifications were made to the cinema in 1961, 1979, during the early 1990s and in 2001. The introduction of multi screens saw the loss of much of its original Art Deco Egyptian styled interior. A close inspection of the exterior of the building shows some period metal and brickwork designs and the pantile roof gives a slight Chinese look. There is also the liberal use of dressed stone in the classical manner giving the frontage some authority. Look also at the side elevations and note the use of tile and brickwork for simple geometrical decoration. Note the louvered window shutter on the top floor.

Tate Library

23. 55-61 STREATHAM HIGH ROAD

This stretch of buildings with shops below is typical of the Edwardian parades built across suburban London. The use of decorative brickwork, dressed stone and decorative gables does much to enhance an otherwise plain façade. Built around 1902. Note the turreted corner with cupola and the Dutch style gables on the front elevation. Also, the brick decorated end gable with a swag decoration.

24. TATE LIBRARY.

Perhaps the most distinctive of the buildings standing in Streatham High Road. A late Victorian building dating to 1890 and blatantly designed in the classical style. The main visual feature is the small copper covered dome supported by squared Doric columns, which also run as a feature of the front façade. Built in Portland stone to the designs of Sidney R.J.Smith, the library was presented to the inhabitants of Streatham by the sugar magnate Sir Henry Tate, of Park Hill, Streatham Common. The building is busy with architectural detail and design. Note the Greek influenced pediment carrying the library name as well as the small columned balustrade and decorated column capitals which give the roof line some movement. Inside the library some of the original decoration can be viewed, although much has been covered with modernisation. One feature, much a symbol of the library, is the clock. This was added to the library in 1912 as the King Edward Memorial Clock and was made by Gillett and Johnston of Croydon. View also the library doors and surround and the memorial stones set into the front wall.

Odeon Cinema

THE HIGH ROAD STREATHAM

55-61 Streatham High Road

25. 65-73 STREATHAM HIGH ROAD.

On the corner of the High Road and Pinfold Road stands a straight forward piece of 1930s architecture, a style seen in many contemporary high streets elsewhere. This building dates to 1934 and replaced some shops built in 1890, which were demolished for road widening. The architecture relies on brick and stonework presented in a streamlined fashion to give visual effect. Note the stepped parapet with a plain central plaque, perhaps missing the date of building. Also the brise-soleil running above the first floor windows. The first floor corner was until the 1950s occupied by the fashionable Zeeta restaurant. The design of this block seems to have been a joint venture with three architects, Bernard George, H. Smith and E. R. Taylor, creating the overall design. Observe the side entrance to the above flats with its period styled canopy.

26. 73A -89 STREATHAM HIGH ROAD.

In stark contrast to the 1930s building with its architectural simplicity, we have, completing this stretch, arguably one of the most decorated buildings to be seen along the High Road. The architectural detail does warrant close observation. The date, 1909, is to be seen on the styled rainwater head, which is one of the ironwork features which make this building. Above the mansard roof, with its pedimented timber windows and arched decoration, runs some very decorative ironwork fashioned in the Arts and Crafts style. The predominant feature is the stone dressing which is emphasised with an octagonal castellated turret marking the corner with Sunnyhill Road. This is reflected in the design for the north end of the block. Note also the decorative stone head of Medusa below the pedimented cornice and broad arched window. Observe the decorative chimney pots.

89 Streatham High Road

73A-89 Streatham High Road

THE HIGH ROAD STREATHAM

27. SUNNYHILL ROAD TO SHRUBBERY ROAD.

Sunnyhill Road was once the village lane leading to Knight's Hill, Norwood. Development in the road has been continuous at the High Road end since medieval times and some early 18th century buildings are disguised behind 19th century fronts. Facing the High Road on the corner of Sunnyhill Road stands a nondescript late Victorian building, its original decorative exterior being lost to cement rendering. However, some decorative brickwork is noticeable on the chimney stacks seen to one side, along with a number of original chimney pots. Next door is a far more interesting building, surviving from the days of Streatham village. Above and behind the shop, now a fast food, outlet is a stuccoed frontage of a late 18th century building. Plain in style save for the cornice on the front elevation. Note the roof style. The building was used as a meeting place by Streatham Parish vestry during the 19th century.

28. STREATHAM POLICE STATION.

Very much the image of a London Police station. Built in 1912, it replaced an earlier building from 1865. The design of the building is credited to John Dixon Butler, who was responsible for the 'typical' style of many London Police stations. It is functional in look and has, as once described, 'a severe yet quite domestic style'. Built in red brick, the main ornamentation relies on dressed stone, particularly around the windows, for visual effect. Observe the entrance with its stone surround and further the pronounced stone cornice which continues as a grand cornice above the second floor. Cube-like and rather imposing on the corner with Shrubbery Road, the station was extended to the rear in 1913. Note the foundation stone by the main entrance and the period styled railings.

29. THE BURTON BUILDING.

Another stylistic Art-Deco building gracing the High Road. Standing next to the Police

Streatham Police Station

97-99 Streatham High Road

Early 19th century house behind 111-113 Streatham High Road

THE HIGH ROAD STREATHAM

The Burton Building

Station on the site formally the Thrale Almshouses, the gentlemen's outfitters, Montague Burton, built the shop in 1932. Designed by Harry Wilson in Burton's 'corporate style'. It is has a front elevation worth some observation with its jazzy 'zig-zag' period decoration plus the stylised elephant heads which decorate the column tops, the main feature of the façade. Also to be seen are the two commemorative stones, dating to 1932 and celebrating the opening of the shop by members of the Burton family. The period shop front has been lost, giving way to a modernist Georgian frontage for the public house called The Goose. Next to Burton's is a small stuccoed building once the home of the pre-Raphaelite painter William Dyce. Below is The Holland Tringham public house, with its brash red frontage of 1920s styling. Note the adjoining early 19th century houses with their small square, upper windows. One has not suffered from later rendering, albeit attractive, and retains its original brick frontage. Built with a plain cornice and standard period styled windows on the first floor. Next are two low rise cottage type properties, which may encase earlier buildings. Observe the stepped gables of the end house. These and the other village buildings would have originally stood behind front gardens.

30. 121 & 123 STREATHAM HIGH ROAD.

These two prominent properties, with their Dutch influenced gables, were originally built for the tailoring business run by George Pratt Jnr. The front elevation is architecturally busy with fashioned brick stonework, swan neck swags above the windows and cornices with decorative ball work. Below the pedimented gable of No. 123 can be seen a stylised plaque giving the date of 1889. Observe the large window area of No. 121, with its patterned glazing bars. This was the clothing showroom. Note a further plaque with the initials G.P. and F.P. Between here and the bank building by Gleneldon Road are four terraced properties, reminiscent of late 18th century ribbon development. These have been rendered in recent years which removed their individual character. Note the remaining sash windows and, in particular, the decorative ironwork finials set above the pilasters with decorated capitals flanking shop No. 133.

121 Streatham High Road

123 Streatham High Road

THE HIGH ROAD STREATHAM

Bank Building

The Dip

31. BANK BUILDING.

Typical looking 19th century bank building. Built in 1883 in a prominent High Road position. The main architectural feature is the rendered ground floor which gives authority to the building. This is further achieved with the use of square and round composite columns and the imposing curved pedimented windows in the design. The entrance is grand in style with its pinky-red granite columns and the mansard roof, with its regular array of dormer widows adding further visual interest. However, over the years the building has lost some of its architectural decoration, notably the curved balustrade over the entrance and the ball finials above the ground floor cornice. To the side of the building in Gleneldon Road can be observed a small red brick property, notable for its Dutch styled gable and bearing the date 1886.

32. THE DIP

The stretch of High Road from the junction of Glenldon Road and Mitcham Lane to approximately Stanthorpe and Gleneagle Roads is locally known as the Dip. The east side was called Bedford Row before suburban development took place. At the top by Gleneldon Road is a 1960s building of three storeys, which stands out of place and with little architectural interest. Following are a group of single storey shops, which have in recent years lost their original shop fronts save for No. 159. These properties predate the rest of this stretch by at least 40 years. Note the original cement cast shop advert on No. 151. The following stretch of buildings down to Stanthorpe Road epitomises the townscape of late Victorian Streatham. There is much architectural and decorative design to see. Built between 1880 and 1890, it is much a variation on a theme, save for No. 177 and adjoining, which are liken to domestic properties, with their tiled brick bay windows with cast capitals and decorated ironwork on the balconies. Similar can be seen further down. The shop No. 177, previously a David Greg grocer's shop, is Grade II listed, due to the original shop interior being extant. Details along this part of the Victorian townscape to observe are the shaped gables, some overtly Dutch or Flemish, which give visual movement as the roof line steps down the hill. Decoration is achieved by using panels of swags and other designs, low relief shaped brickwork, bands of stonework, ball finials on the roofline and brick patterned chimney stacks. Note between the shops the pink granite pilasters, some with decorated capitals, and the scrolled design feature above. Above No.193 is a fine example of Victorian

Gleneldon Mews

THE HIGH ROAD STREATHAM

213c Streatham High Road

225 Streatham High Road

decorative ironwork made for a shop sign. Observe the date panels. The sequence is finished with a corner building at Stanthorpe Road. This building has some interesting features, notably the arcade styled decorative balcony, glazing bars and the extended chimney stacks to the first floor.

33. GLENELDON MEWS

To the rear of these buildings is Gleneldon Mews containing stables and carriage sheds, of which some good examples still survive. A feature of the mews is the granite cobbled road surface.

The High Road between Stanthorpe Road and Hopton Road has been substantially raised to make an approach way and bridge over the railway line built during 1866-1868. This section of buildings is primarily late Victorian, built as part of the developing town centre.

34. 213c STREATHAM HIGH ROAD.

The Stanthorpe Road corner was dominated until 1966 by the Streatham Methodist church, built in 1882. A new building, a remodelling of a plain three storey brick structure built in the late 1960s, marks the site. This pleasing new building, with its gabled end and dormer windows, reflects the surrounding styles. The adjoining properties again reflect domestic architecture, and are much a repeat of those seen along the Dip.

35. BEDFORD PARK HOTEL.

A quality building in this stretch is the Bedford Park Hotel, built in 1882. The main feature to observe is the gable with its decorative boarding imitating traditional 'Tudorbethan' styles, popular at the time. Decorative details to be seen are moulded floral decoration, decorated brackets and window lintels. A further feature is the ironwork at ground level. Note the slim barley twist iron pillars, the 'Saloon' signs and the narrow mosaic panels by the entrance doors. In contrast, next door No. 225, is an early 1950s building, originally a post office, and designed reflecting the austerity of the post war years. It replaced the Empire Cinema destroyed by a Flying Bomb in the second world war.

The Bedford Park Public House

THE HIGH ROAD STREATHAM

Queen's Parade

Art Deco Clock on Century House

36. QUEEN'S PARADE.

The following group of buildings is known as Queen's Parade, built 1882-1900. The decoration relies on leafy styled pargetting seen under the eaves and gables, notably on the end block. The styled dormer windows give interest to the roofline. Note the very decorative name panel, decorative tile cladding and also the original sash windows above No. 239. The architects were Wheeler and Holland. The archway seen by No. 227 was the original entrance to Russell's footpath before the building of the railway which cut the path. Following is Bridge Parade, a row of plain lockup shops built during the 1920s. No. 5 has the original shop front.

37. HOPTON HOUSE.

Passing the steps to Russell's footpath is Hopton House, a modern building dating to the 1980s and presently used as council offices. A functional building with little decoration, save for brick column like features, dormer widows and horizontal rows of windows. Next is Hopton Parade, another group of lockup shops with some minimal period design and dating to the 1920s.

38. CENTURY HOUSE, 245 STREATHAM, HIGH ROAD.

Standing with some majesty on the corner of Hopton Road is Century House. Typically Art-Deco in style. This modernistic thirties building was built in 1938 as the headquarters for James Walker, the jewellers and silversmiths. It was also their showroom and manufacturing base for their chain of retail shops. It was one of the first buildings to incorporate an underground car park. As can be observed, the main feature of the building is the stone clad central block which faces the High Road. This is dramatised with the long vertical window arrangement bringing light into the central staircase. At ground level, a band of black granite panelling, with some black ceramic coping tiles by the entrance, runs from the main block around to the workshop and office area in Hopton Road. Here can be seen the bulk of the building with its architectural emphasis on the horizontal line with stone stringing and the window line. Note the large Art Deco clock, a Streatham icon, and the flight of steps with the period handrails leading to the styled entrance. Note the granite cornerstone bearing the date of building. Prior to the sale of the building, a small decorative garden with a post and rail fence lay by the entrance, but since taken up for an enlarged pavement. The steps leading to the garden have survived. Following closure of the business in 1984, the building was converted into luxury flats.

Hopton House

THE HIGH ROAD STREATHAM

Century House

END OF THE CONSERVATION AREA.

39. ALBERT CARR GARDENS.

A large housing estate dominating the High Road junction with Streatham Common North Side. Before these gardens are reached, there is a block of flats set back from the High Road. Built in the 1960s and approached from Polworth Road, they replaced two large late Victorian mansions. Built by Wandsworth Borough Council during the 1950s. Previously the site of Coventry Hall and earlier one of the Streatham manor houses. The estate comprises of seven large blocks set between green areas. Of plain design with minimal decoration but nevertheless an attractive collection of buildings. Some stonework stringing and raised brick coursing along the ground floor. Note the second floor walkways with their period iron railings and the new contemporary styled, 'wavy-line' railings on the boundary wall.

BEGINNING OF THE STREATHAM COMMON CONSERVATION AREA (CA43)

40. STREATHAM MEMORIAL GARDENS.

The Streatham War Memorial was designed by Albert T. Toft and the gardens opened in 1922. Also in the gardens can be seen the Civilian War memorial erected in 2006. The simplicity of this limestone memorial, designed by Ekkehard Attenburger, stands in contrast to Toft's traditional design.

Streatham War Memorial with Albert Carr Gardens at the rear.

THE HIGH ROAD STREATHAM

325 Streatham High Road and Hilldown Court

41. STREATHAM COMMON,

Once the manorial wastes of South Streatham Village. Declared a Conservation Area in 1994. Note the two plain brick keepers' huts dating to about 1912. Recently re-roofed, with original chimney stacks and pots remaining. The pond was originally a natural feature fed by drainage from top of the common. Converted into a paddling pond by the London County Council in 1939. Except for resurfacing, the pond retains it original form. Nearby stood the horse trough. This was removed from the High Road opposite Greyhound Lane to its present position at the top of the common for road widening during 1974.

42. VOSS COURT.

Originally the site and grounds of Streatham Court. Developed by W. Mason the builders in 1909 and by W.J.F.Gillett. Houses built in 1924. A petrol station and garage were built in 1928 by Miller and Sons and known as the Renown Garage. This garage has seen a number of re-developments, the most recent dating to the early 2000s. In the garage forecourt stood the 7th milestone from London which was removed during modernisation of the garage in the mid 1970s. The 1924 houses are to be seen behind the garage.

END OF THE CONSERVATION AREA.

43. BOSCOMBE GARDENS.

Boscombe Gardens, built in 1983, replaced some large Victorian mansions. Brick built with no decoration but visually attractive with enclosed balconies, garden walls and set behind a green verge with mature trees.

44. RYAN COURT.

Dominating the south corner of Baldry Gardens is Ryan Court, an imposing group of six residential blocks and a Health Centre. Built during the 1970s, the blocks were refurbished to their present state in 2004. This has given the blocks a striking appearance through the use of external cladding and new sweeping curved roofs. The overall appearance is metallic and airport looking.

45. SPA HOUSE

Next in a softer style of architecture is the recently built Spa House. Also referred to as Spa Central, this residential block has architectural appeal with its modern frontage of contrasting brick and cement rendering. Visually interesting with the 1950s styling of the tower. Attractive balconies, girder and tubular styled. Behind is Coulthurst Court.

46. HEYBRIDGE AVENUE TO HILLDOWN ROAD.

The corner building, No. 325, has lost much of its originality with the brickwork being painted white. However, note the Dutch styled gable with its

Ryan Court

THE HIGH ROAD STREATHAM

357-367 Streatham High Road

curved lines and ball top finial and the decorative floral tile frieze running below. Some decorative brickwork has been left unpainted and is worth a look. Note the mansard roof and the ribs projecting down from the curvy gable, and the decorative course work linking the window arches. The shop front is a modern addition. Adjoining is a pleasing block of flats called Hilldown Court. Built 1935 by Albert Soden of Streatham. Advertised as having modern kitchens with first class equipment, refrigerators, electric fires, instant hot water, marble fireplaces and modern decorative schemes. The block is noticeable by its tile-hung bay windows set at each end. Stone stringing above the windows on the ground and first floor break up the plainness of the brickwork. Note the roof and dormer windows, the brickwork of the parapets on the second floor and the styled front wall of the court. Next is Douglas Robinson Court. Standard looking late 1950s block of flats built by Wandsworth Borough Council. A glazed stair well is the main feature of the brick frontage along with the period entrance below. Note the pantile roof and outside brick wall with tile coping.

47. HILLDOWN ROAD TO HEATHDENE ROAD.

This stretch is filled with two blocks of flats, Nos. 357 to 367, built by Wandsworth Borough Council in the same style as Douglas Robinson House and at the same time. Replaced Coulthurst Cottages,

48. SINCLAIR COURT

On the corner with Heathdene Road is a modern development, Sinclair Court, built in 2007. Much use is made of modern material and architectural design. Note the use of wood cladding, and the stepped roofline and styled metal balconies. A pleasing building, not out of keeping. Leading into Green Lane are some houses of late Edwardian date. From here to beyond Hermitage Lane, the properties have been demolished to make way for anticipated development. Demolition included the loss of The King William IV Public House, which stood between Green Lane and Hermitage Lane. Two lamp post bases from the outside wall of the public house remain by the pavement.

49 HERMITAGE LANE TO NORBURY BORDER

Further on Nos. 339 to 441, which date to about 1890, stand out amongst this stretch of buildings, having the look of a house with its hipped roof, decorative window lintels and use of red and yellow brick. Next is a long building which takes the curve in the road. Single storey and built about 1920. Some limited use of decorative brickwork, noticeable with the arches above the front entrance doors. Note the design of the doors. Following this is a row of lock-up shops, replacing Hermitage Bridge Cottages about 1910. Next is a cottagey looking property with a double gabled roof and bays windows. Has seen better days but still looks attractive under the present coat of white. Here is Hermitage Bridge and the River Graveney which mark the boundary between Streatham and Norbury, Lambeth and Croydon, and the London – Surrey border until 1965.

Sinclair Court

THE HIGH ROAD STREATHAM

Streatham High Road - West Side

Crown and Sceptre Public House

50. CROWN AND SCEPTRE PUBLIC HOUSE.

A detached building, with two angled bay windows which dominate the frontage. Above these are short lengths of balustrade which gives some decoration to otherwise plain window bays. Most of the decoration is on the ground floor where the exuberant use of ceramic tiles gives a 'pubbish' but a pleasing effect. Note the arched windows with their moulded decoration and crown, and the pillared entrance. Plenty to look at with this building. View the side elevation in Streatham Place and note the decorated columns of the entrance. The building dates to 1822 with alterations made during the 1870s. Found its present look during the early 20th century. Refurbished in 2002.

51. STAPLEFIELD CLOSE (CLAREMONT ESTATE WEST).

The look and style of the three blocks that make Staplefield Close reflect the austerity that followed the second world war. Built by Wandsworth Borough Council in 1955. Constructed in yellow stock brick and with flat roofs. Functional looking buildings with recessed balconies and extended stair wells. Plain elevations save for architraves around windows. Later additions were made to this estate from the late 1960s with the addition of three blocks. Chipstead House has a pitched roof with pantiles, glazed stair well to one end and covered walkways to flats; Coulsdon House is similar. Note the protruding glazed stair well at the far end. Tierney Terrace, which is in Tierney Road, is a single storey block attractively presented with a weatherboard frontage; dates to the 1960s.

Staplefield Close (Claremont Estate West)

THE HIGH ROAD STREATHAM

Today the estate is called the Claremont Estate, and included into the council development seen on the opposite side of the High Road.

52. THE PARAGON.

A housing development of the late Regency period which stretched along the High Road from approximately Streatham Place to Telford Avenue. By the late 1940s, most of the houses had been demolished for post-war house building. Nos. 40, 42 and 44 are the surviving villas from this early development. They are listed as buildings of architectural interest. Of the two houses, No. 44 is the most interesting. It has a classical style frontage emphasised with a Doric fluted columned entrance porch. Note the Gothic style glazing bars. Slate roof. Much of the original interior of this property has survived.

Nos. 40 and 42 adjoining have similar visual attributes. Following is Conway House, a three storey block of flats. Plain looking with no commendable style. Brick built with some rough cast rendering on the elevations. On the High Road side at ground level a decorative screen of pre-cast concreted blocks conceals an open area. Entrance to the block is in Telford Avenue. Built during the 1970s.

44 Streatham Hill

BEGINNING OF THE CONSERVATION AREA (CA54).
From Telford Avenue to approximately Natal Road.

53. TELFORD PARADE MANSIONS.

When approaching from London the four-storey Telford Parade Mansions gives a visual introduction to 1930s townscape of Streatham. Designed by Frank Verity, Beverley and Horner in 1935 the mansions are simple in design with the curved north end emphasised with plain balconies. With the absence of decoration, save for the balconies, the building imparts

Telford Parade Mansions

THE HIGH ROAD STREATHAM

Telford Court

a streamlined appearance. Some minor brick patterning above the windows and one original shop part remain. Note the entrance and contemporary lettering for name. Around the corner in Telford Avenue can be seen Telford Avenue Mansions. Dating to the same year and designed by the same architects, these mansions show more contemporary styling. Note the Art Deco styled entrances with 'sunburst' iron railings set above, contemporary signage and the unusual tapered chimneys. The building shows influence from ancient Egypt. Front boundary wall still stands.

54. TELFORD COURT.

West End architecture in Streatham. Built in 1931 and designed by Frank Harrington. Four shallow bays and lengthy balconies break the frontage. Very little decoration. Plain keystones above Georgian looking windows along the second floor. White rendering highlights the long shop frontage, which is broken by two simple arched entrances to the flats above. Note the period styled doors with their metalwork and original signage. The main features of this development are the belvederes which dominate the roofline. With their pantile roofs, they impart a Mediterranean look.

55. WYATT PARK MANSIONS.

Part of the long parade of 1930s building, these mansions are plain looking. The frontage is broken by columns of white rendered bay windows and decoration is left to the brick pattern quoins on the corners of the two shallow wings. Note the styled entrance with original wooden doors and signage. The architects were H. J. S. Abrams and Sons; and built in 1937.

56. STREATHAM HILL THEATRE (RIVA BINGO HALL).

A 1920s version of classical architecture. Bold and bright with the frontage cased in Doulton's Carrara tiles. Designed by William George Sprague and William Henry Barton, the 2,500 seat theatre opened for performances in 1929. Was one of the largest theatres outside the West End of London. The focus of the facade is the large loggia styled area which is fronted by a row of plain Doric columns.

Wyatt Park Mansions

THE HIGH ROAD STREATHAM

Riva Bingo the former Streatham Hill Theatre Building

Beneath a plain pediment on each wing are moulded wreaths. Note also the shallow pilaster with their suggested capitals on the wings, the Roman styled railings between the columns, the pantile roof plus the decorated parapet. The lavish and exuberant foyer and auditorium area has survived. Many famous actors have performed at the theatre, which closed in 1962. Later it re-opened as a Bingo Hall. It is a Grade II listed building. Damage suffered from a V1 Flying Bomb in 1944 can be seen in the new looking brickwork in Barrhill Road. The foundation plaque laid by Eveleyn Laye in 1929 can be seen on the front wall, to the left of the entrance.

57. BARHILL TO ARDWELL ROAD.

A plain looking development which dates to the mid 1930s. The main feature of the frontage is the stone central block, with pairs of balconies decorated with stylistic iron work. The remainder of the block is brickwork, which in places is used for decoration, i.e. quoins. Plain stone dressing around the windows and above the two end wings. Interesting roofline and ends. Note the chimney stacks.

58. GAUMONT PALACE CINEMA (MEGABOWL).

Like the nearby theatre, the building has a sense of grandeur. The rectangular frontage has a large central

Interior of Riva Bingo the former Streatham Hill Theatre Building

25

THE HIGH ROAD STREATHAM

Megabowl the former Gaumont Palace Cinema

loggia, formalised by large windows with classical pediments. Fronting this are six fluted Doric columns, with four being placed as pairs. This area was used as an open-air terrace for refreshments and was floodlit during the evenings. Flanking the centre are two brick wings with little decoration, except for vertical lines of raised brickwork highlighting the windows. At ground level, the brickwork is rendered and lined to give the effect of stonework. Note the stone cornice on the two wings and the decorated parapet. The cinema opened in 1932 and was designed by Charles Nicholas and J. E. Dixon-Spain. Held an audience of just over 2,400 people. During the second world war, the building suffered from bomb damage and the interior was badly damaged. Rebuilt to the designs of T.P. Bennett & Son and re-opened in 1955 with reduced seating capacity. Closed shortly after in 1961. Became a 36-lane Top Rank Bowling Alley in 1962, and later the Megabowl in 1988. Currently closed.

59. CAESAR'S (LOCARNO BALL ROOM).

Nothing particular about this stretch of architecture, which incorporates a dance hall which

Caesars the former Locarno Ballroom

THE HIGH ROAD STREATHAM

Streatham Hill Station

opened in 1929. The main feature is the two storey central block which is presented in part brick and stone style cladding, but this is mostly obscured by the overbearing Roman Chariot springing from a flashy modern frontage. The adjacent single storey blocks and two storey wings are plain with stone dressing around the windows. Minimum brick decoration and simple pitched roofs. Note the entrance to the flats above with their styled window. Originally built as Lutie's ballroom in 1929 and designed by Trehearne and Norman Preston & Co. Acquired by Mecca in 1931. However, it has been recorded as being built by Mecca Works Department, E. J. White – perhaps a modernisation of the dance hall. The dance hall was a popular venue during the 1950s and the 1960s and over the years has been named the 'Cats Whisker's' (1969), 'The Studio' (1984), 'The Ritzy' (1990) and 'Caesars' (1995). A side entrance led to the famous 'Stork Club', closed in the 1960s. Contributed to the reputation of Streatham being called the 'entertainment centre of South London'.

60. ARBORFIELD HOUSE CORNER.

Standing on the corner of Sternhold Avenue and the High Road (Nos. 172 to 178) is a well designed commercial and residential building, restrained in its decoration and dated to just before the 1920s. The main element in the design is the five sided turret-looking feature designed into the corner. This is capped with a cupola supported by scrolled consoles and topped with a large spike shape finial. Note the decorative arches and keystones above the windows. Another strong feature to appreciate is the pediment styled gables with their dentil decoration, which continues as a cornice along the building. Observe the decorative brickwork at the bottom of the gables, above the windows elsewhere and, in particular, the steps to the rear of the building in Sternhold Avenue. The original building on the site was Arborfield House, which was set back from the High Road, and destroyed in a Zeppelin bombing raid in 1916.

61. STREATHAM HILL STATION.

Looks nothing like a railway station. This barn like building, which is of iron construction and faced with timber, was a concession to those who resented the new railway architecture. Built in 1856 as a ticket hall for the West End of London & Crystal Palace Railway. A plain and functional design. Note the decorative iron brackets which support the low overhanging roof. Has the

178 Streatham Hill

Streatham Hill Station Shop

Stonehill Mansions

original sash window. Much of the original interior has gone although the stairs to the platform keep some of their period design. Note the timber architraves around the doors and window. To the side of the station, down Sternhold Avenue, is a row of lock up shops dating to the late 19th century. Some still carry original decorative features. View the rear of these buildings from Drewstead Road and note the manner of their construction. Unusual buildings.

62. STONEHILL MANSIONS.

One of the best architectural frontages along the High Road. Running from Drewstead Road towards Broadlands Avenue and built on the site of a large house called Stonehills. Designed by the architects Meech and Goodall in 1905. This building is worth a very good look. There is much to see. Note the Doric pilasters, the Dutch influenced gable with its Venetian windows, the use of dentil decoration along the cornice, the ribbed cupolas at each corner, the windows with their rounded pediments and shallow bay windows. The mansard roof is slated with small decorative circular window features set below a rounded pediments. Note also the boldly designed entrances to the above flats. Original signage. Plenty of stucco work. View side elevation in Drewstead Road, particularly the metalwork on the entrance door.

63. BROADLAND MANSIONS.

Standard looking 1930s design. Stretching from Nos. 24 to 36. Little obvious decoration, however the mixed use of red and yellow brickwork has a visual effect. Angled corner end with decorative brickwork which is repeated along the front and side elevations. A plain looking parapet with some simple shaping. Original bank frontage remains on the corner with Broadlands Avenue. The block marks the site of Broadlands House.

Broadlands Mansions

THE HIGH ROAD STREATHAM

52-58 Streatham High Road

64. TESCO EXPRESS, 42 STREATHAM HIGH ROAD

On the corner of the High Road and Broadlands Avenue is a Tesco Express supermarket opened in December 2007. The frontage has no visual merit. This single storey building was originally a Temperance Billiard Hall, built circa 1910.

65. 52-58 STREATHAM HIGH ROAD

Standing in complete contrast, is arguably one of the best designed buildings along the High Road. Nos. 52 to 58, built circa 1914 reflects the mood of the Arts and Crafts movement. The design is well balanced with two overhanging gables at each end. Below are double bays with canopy styled swept roofs, emphasised by being painted black. The use of coloured brick and brickwork designs impart a graceful appearance to the central frontage. Note the Georgian look about the dormer windows set in the steeply pitched roof. Observe the narrow round headed windows at each end on the top floor and the stone entrance with its classical design.

66. HORSE AND GROOM

The next cluster of buildings includes the Horse and Groom public house. The origin of this building dates back to 1717 and was known as the 'Halfway House'. Was one of the principal coaching stops in Streatham on the road to and from London. Quite a pleasing building but recently lost its charm with the white washing of the exterior. Brick built with a pronounced central gable flanked by pairs of pointed tiled dormer windows. Some decorative brickwork can be seen. Built around 1865.

Tesco Express, 42 Streatham High Road

Horse and Groom Public House

THE HIGH ROAD STREATHAM

Belle Vue Terrace, 62-70 Streatham High Road

67. BELLE VUE TERRACE, 62-70 STREATHAM HIGH ROAD

Adjoining properties, Nos. 62 to 70, are of a similar build and date. Note the Tudor style moulding over the windows and the pointed gables of the last three.

68. DE MONTFORD PARADE.

Following in the same stretch are two very pleasing buildings of quality design with neo-classical frontages. The two storey building has a simple classical frontage, using elegant pilasters with Ionic capitals, complimented by a decorated pediment at each end and linked by a plain cornice. The building has good proportions. One of the finer buildings along the High Road. Adjoining is a single storey block of complimentary design with some Art Deco elements in the decoration. The design is expressed with well spaced pilasters topped with Doric capitals which break up the straightforward brickwork. Minimal decoration relies on panels with chain-like designs set above the windows. Fluted urns decorate the parapet. The angled corner entrance to the building carries the name plaque beneath the cornice. Built during the mid-1930s to the design of the architect Henry Braddock. Site of De Montfort House demolished in 1933.

69. 76 STREATHAM HIGH ROAD

No. 76 is an attractive corner building. The main feature is the turreted end, formalised at roof level and finished with a most pleasing octagonal timber lantern. Note the shaped gable with its ball finial, the well shaped oriel windows with tiled roof, and the stone string course linking the arched windows on the first floor; also the rainwater heads by the bay windows. Original shop front remains on the corner.

76 Streatham High Road

De Montfort Parade

THE HIGH ROAD STREATHAM

Next, there is a gap in the building sequence, which is filled by a shop, No. 78a, with balustrade above. The architecture of Gordon Mansions, which continues the sequence, offers just a long plain façade with arched first floor windows and stone stringing giving some visual interest. This section culminates in a turreted corner block, similar to that described above. This stretch was built around 1905.

70. NORFOLK HOUSE ROAD TO KINGSCOURT ROAD.

On the corner of this section, at Kingscourt Road and at Norfolk House Road, are turreted properties, much similar in

Turrets at the High Road junction with Kingscourt Road

design and style to the building seen previously. This section offers more architectural interest – it is better designed. The main feature is the central section with the two white gables. Note the large dormer windows. Again, the use of exaggerated keystones and stone stringing livens up the frontage and the side elevations of the end buildings. Dated to the late 1890s.

71. KINGSCOURT ROAD TO WOODBOURNE AVENUE.

On the High Road corner a turreted building of Edwardian date. In the same style as opposite. Adjoining are a number of single-storey shops, dating to the mid 1920s. No

130 Streatham High Road site of former Golden Domes Cinema

particular style, save the balustrade that runs above the shops.

72. 130 STREATHAM HIGH ROAD

Next is the old Golden Domes cinema, No. 130, of which only the auditorium, dating to 1927, remains and can be seen behind the modern shop front. The cinema was built in 1912 to the designs of G. A. Boswell and closed in 1938.

73. 134 STREATHAM HIGH ROAD FORMER POST OFFICE

Next to this and marking the corner is the Telephone Exchange, a fine, sturdy looking building with classical designs. The gable is highlighted with a small Venetian window, and a small obelisk rising from a broken pediment at the apex. Note the strong style of the windows, the dentilated cornice which runs around the building above the first floor and the brick and stone detail above the rainwater or hopper heads. These metalwork features carry the date 1909.

The section between Woodbourne and Becmead Avenues was built during the 1900s and starts off and ends with a turreted building at each end. Unfortunately, the architectural integrity along here has been broken with the insertion of the Woolworth and W.H. Smith buildings.

Former Streatham Post Office with Telephone Exchange above

138 Streatham High Road

156-178 Streatham High Road

74. 138 STREATHAM HIGH ROAD

On the corner with Woodbourne Avenue, No. 138, the turret is finished with an oriental styled cupola. Note the unusual styled gable set into a mansard roof and the varied window styles of this property, also the shallow brick pilasters with simple capitals above the entrance. The entrance has a pair of windows separating the arched pediment from the classical styled doorway; original wooden doors.

75. WOOLWORTHS, 148-154 STREATHAM HIGH ROAD

Adjoining is the two storey Woolworth building, built during the late 1950s. Has a 'Festival of Britain' style about it. Modernistic and out of keeping with its architectural surrounds.

76. 156-178 STREATHAM HIGH ROAD

The following stretch is generally unfussy in style and relies mostly on symmetry. The most noticeable features are the windows with their stone surrounds and elongated keystones. Interesting parapet with semi-circular design. Straightforward gables highlighted in places with a shell motif. Note the two large gables with Celtic cross designs and the bay windows which relieve the flatness of this long façade.

77. W H SMITH, 180-182 STREATHAM HIGH ROAD

Adjoining was Sharman's drapers shop, now W.H.Smith, Nos. 180-182. This frontage is dated to 1929 and is all Art Deco. Geometrical in look with emphasis on the vertical and horizontal line. Two large vertical windows each divided with two horizontal metal panels sporting Art Deco motif. Note the stepped pediment carrying the name of the original shop. Next, on the corner, is an Edwardian property, turreted with a cupola. Regular design for the period with no outstanding features. Between Becmead Avenue and Prentis Road there is a continuous stretch of varied architecture, with little cohesion between styles. However, plenty of fancy brickwork and moulding to enjoy. On the corner of the Avenue stands a plain building with average decoration. Some decorative brickwork below the gables and panels containing swags. The gables are neat in their design.

Woolworths, 146-154 Streatham High Road

180-182 Streatham High Road

THE HIGH ROAD STREATHAM

Iceland, 194-198 Streatham High Road

North Parade, 200-208 Streatham High Road

Note the rounded pediment above the window on the top floor. This building group is finished with an octagonal end turret, in keeping with the opposite corner of the avenue. Built by William Mason in 1900, probably to the designs of E. B. Lanson.

78. ICELAND, 194-198 STREATHAM HIGH ROAD

Next is perhaps the most unattractive building along the High Road. A two storey façade of sheet metal with vertical ribbing. The façade is broken by a narrow row of windows. At present a freezer supermarket. Built on the site of Sparrow Hall.

79. NORTH PARADE, 200-208 STREATHAM HIGH ROAD

The look of the following row of premises is quite the opposite. The brick decorated panel gives the date of 1888. Again, the use of swags, stone stringing and styled gables in the Dutch manner adds visual interest. Note the very decorative arched entrance between the shops with its pediment, finials and consoles, plus the decorative stonework and the name 'North Parade'. Historically this part of the High Road was the end of the village.

80. 210-224 STREATHAM HIGH ROAD

The next stretch, Nos. 210 – 224, is the long brick façade built in 1996 to the designs of Tripe and Wakeham, the architects. Plain looking and offering some acceptance of the traditional townscape in the overall design. Simple gables and stone dressings offer decoration. The bay windows give some life to the architecture. The site was formerly Pratts department store, the largest shop in Streatham, which closed in 1990 and resulted in the demolition of some fine mid-Victorian premises. Adjoining is a 1930s tiled covered building with some minimum Art Deco styling. Perhaps behind is an 18th century building.

210-224 Streatham High Road, former site of Pratts

North Parade

33

THE HIGH ROAD STREATHAM

230 Streatham High Road.

The White Lion

81. 230 STREATHAM HIGH ROAD

Next door is No. 230, a small plain looking two storey property. This is the only building on this side of the High Road surviving from Streatham village and dated to the early 19th century. Note the stone architrave around the windows and the roughed keystone with supporting scrolls - plus the surviving shop front.

82. THE WHITE LION

In contrast, standing next door is the White Lion public house. Marks the site of a number of earlier buildings. This architecturally busy looking building comes from the designs of F. Gough & Co and dates to 1895. The elaborateness of this fine looking building is seen in the arched windows, ornamental keystones, stone string courses, decorative brickwork and moulding and the busy looking gables with their pointed finials. The main feature is the central section dominated by the bay windows and the tall Elizabethan looking chimney stacks. Truly an imposing façade. Note the two-tone granite pilasters with their composite capitals at street level and original shop front by the service entrance. Note the decorative glazing bars of the shop and windows along the frontage. The next section leading to Prentis Road dates to 1889, and is visually similar to that seen previously. Built by William Mason of Streatham.

83. SOUTH LONDON LIBERAL SYNAGOGUE, PRENTIS ROAD.

The South London Liberal Synagogue building was part of Streatham College for Girls and was known as Lady Tate Hall. Opened in 1909, closed in 1933 and becoming a synagogue in 1938. Designed by Sidney Smith. Has a simple but attractive frontage with decorative brick quoins and

The White Lion

South London Liberal Synagogue

window surrounds. The dentilated stone cornice which moves to create a pediment adds some character, as does the square semi-classical entrance. Note the extended keystones. To the left of the main entrance is the foundation stone.

84. STREATHAM POST SORTING OFFICE, PRENTIS ROAD.

Not to be missed is Streatham postal sorting office. Built about 1911. The most noticeable feature is the fine pointed pediment enclosing a well carved Royal Coat of Arms. This sits above an impressive curved window. Below a rounded pediment, complimented with decorative stonework, marks the entrance. In all an attractive building. Plenty of stonework to look at. The decorative wall and railings outside were removed some years ago.

85. 248-252 STREATHAM HIGH ROAD

This stretch of buildings between Prentis Road and St. Leonard's Church loses it continuity with the insertion of a later styled building. Nevertheless, there are interesting feature to see. From Prentis Road the buildings are straightforward in style and decoration. Again stone stringing adds decoration and the gables are plain. However, one feature gives interest – the mock Tudor frontage to the first floor of No. 250, with its beams, carved wood and tiled canopy, circa 1930s. Part of the house style of Dorothy Perkins shops. Note the granite pilasters topped with styled consoles each side of No. 252.

86 CENTRAL PARADE

Sandwiched between this Victorian shopping parade is a totally different building, Central Parade, with its architectural emphasis on the horizontal line. Built on the site of an old house called The Shrubbery. Designed by Dixon and Braddock in the modernistic style and built in 1934. Two storeys in height with stylish decoration using cast cement. Note the deep cornice running above the second floor, below which runs stylish leaf-design frieze, and other period styling which makes this building one of the more interesting interwar buildings.

87. 254-268 STREATHAM HIGH ROAD

The following 19th century buildings in this section rely on decorative stonework stringing and raised brickwork. Note the squared pilasters dividing the windows and the stepped gable. Designed by John S. Quilter and built by a local builder William Mason in 1901. The corner block facing the church was originally a bank. Note the stepped gable and cupola.

Streatham Post Sorting Office

Central Parade

250 Streatham High Road

88. ST. LEONARD'S PARISH CHURCH.

A church of Saxon foundation. Recorded in the Domesday Book of 1086. There have been many additions and alterations to the church over the centuries. The church building we see today is largely a Victorian creation. The oldest part is the tower, dating to the mid-14th century, encased within the present building. The main part of the building, seen rendered in 'roman cement' dates to a rebuild undertaken during 1831 and 1832 by J. Parkinson. The remainder, which is in stone, was added by Benjamin Ferrey and dates to the mid-1860s. Following a disastrous fire in 1975, the nave was rebuilt to the designs of Douglas Feast and Partners. Very little of the Victorian interior has survived. Some medieval and later monuments, the medieval font, plus the exterior flint and stone walls of the old tower are to be seen inside. Note the flint dressing of the tower and the buttresses, which are medieval. Outside, note the gracefully designed broach spire, which is nearly 130 feet in height, and the weather vane. Also, the various window styles, particularly those of the nave, with their geometrical tracery. The building is Grade II listed. Also explore the graveyard, where notable Streatham people are buried, e.g. William Dyce RA and Sir Arthur Helps. View the rather time worn Coadstone tomb of Joseph Hay, dated 1808, and other fine tombs. Close to the church is the Church Hall, dated to 1908. An Arts and Crafts styled building. Note the use of decorative brickwork above the side entrance and the general design of the building, particularly the style of the roofs.

St. Leonard's Church

Church of the English Martyrs

89. CHURCH OF THE ENGLISH MARTYRS.

The church stands on the corner of Mitcham Lane and Tooting Bec Gardens. Designed and presented in the medieval style of French Gothic. Grade II* listed. This fine building was designed by A. E. Purdie and built between 1892 and 1896 by Hill Brothers and W.H.Lorden of Tooting. Opened in May 1894. There is much to see in the architecture of this building. For example, the tower and broach spire, buttresses, statuary, the ornate main entrance and the lancet windows with their decorated columns. Also the decorative iron railings around the church. The spire is just under 137 feet in height. Observe the highly decorated wrought iron weathervane. To the side of the church, in Tooting Bec Gardens, is a small building in similar style, built as an electricity sub-station and dates from 1896 to the designs of a local architect, Frederick Wheeler. This is Grade II listed. Note the decorative hinges to the door of this building and the rainwater head and pipe. Next door to the left of the church is the Presbytery, also Grade II listed. A pleasing building to view, with its attractive oriel window, the gable with its stone decoration and decorative arch. Note the carvings and stonework above the entrance. Dated to the 1900s. Adjoining is a plain building with minimal decoration, except for the iron work on the balcony. Built during the 1930s as a church hall. To the rear of the church in Tooting Bec Gardens is a winged building, conservative in design with attractive dormer windows. Probably built during the 1920s.

90. MOSQUE, FORMERLY STREATHAM FIRE STATION.

Most of the original frontage remains, including the large, four panelled fire tender doors. Built for the London County Council in 1903. Not over decorated, but has a prominent curved pediment with a short mansard roof adjoining. To the right is a modern low building marking that part of the station destroyed by bombing in 1940. Note the original metal drill tower standing at the station. Ceased to be a fire station in 1971.

91. THE CRESCENT, MITCHAM LANE.

Terrace type properties of two storeys dating to 1891. Visually interesting with decorative windows and pargetting, with the date seen above No. 12. Note the bay frontage to No. 16 and the terracotta name on No. 10. Some brick patterning, noticeably just beneath the roof. Similar styles and influences can been seen in the building along the Dip, the Broadway and the Triangle, approaching Streatham Station. Much decoration and styling to observe.

92. THE MANOR ARMS, MITCHAM LANE.

A blockish looking building filling the corner with Babington Road. Built in 1925 and taking its name from a previous 18th century building. The main

South London Islamic Centre

features are the many windows and the domed extension, which fills the apex of the corner. Little eternal decoration, save for some raised brick courses, and the large tile course around the building. Note the roof style and dormer windows, the decorative iron balcony and tall chimneys.

93. THE CORNER BLOCK, MITCHAM LANE.

Another good example of period architecture. This block, dating to the mid 1930s, replaced a Victorian development, including the old market building, which were demolished for road widening. The development, Nos. 270 to 290, was designed by T. P. Bennett & Sons with a streamlined look and successfully covers the gradient of the Dip as it steps down towards Streatham Green. The end elevation by the Green is geometrical with horizontal brick banding giving minimum decoration to an otherwise plain elevation. Note the line of red bricks echoing the angled gable. The High Road frontage is balanced at each end with three pairs of squared bay windows. Coloured brick stringing, shaped cornice, cement cast octagons and geometric work give unity to the three centre stepped blocks, particularly the long narrow canopies above the second floors. The rounded north end contrasts with the surrounding buildings with its rows of bay windows and the large octagonal decorative wooden lantern with its louvered sides and pantile base. Follow the architecture around into Mitcham Lane where the

Manor Arms Public House

THE HIGH ROAD STREATHAM

original shop fronts have more or less survived. Here, attached to this block is a terrace of three properties dating to the 1890s. Note the stepped entrances with their fluted pilasters each side and their decorated capitals. Observe the brick decoration at No. 9 and chimney stack. Note the decorative iron railings and the steps on the corner of the High Road and Mitcham Lane, built to offset the difference in pavement heights.

94. DYCE FOUNTAIN, STREATHAM GREEN.

The Green is a relic of the medieval village of Streatham. Note the original 19th century iron railings along the High Road side. The fountain was designed by William Dyce, the Pre-Raphaelite painter and a resident of Streatham. Originally stood opposite the parish church at the junction of the High Road with Mitcham Lane. Erected there 1862 and moved to its present position in 1933. Designed in the Gothic revival style, popular at the time. Architectural looking and not over decorated, mixed use of stone.

95. THE BROADWAY

A sweep of commercial properties built 1883-4 and 1893 running from Streatham Green into Gleneagle Road. Again, there is much to see and appreciate in this architectural group, such as original sash windows, plaster and terracotta work. Plenty of fancy brick detail and shaped gables. Much of the decoration comes from the skilled use of brickwork seen above and around the windows. The roofline is broken with a mixture of Queen Anne or Dutch styled gables indicative of the architecture seen in this part of the High Road. The first building next to the Green is visually interesting with its use of brick and decoration. Observe the end elevation overlooking the green with its decorated chimney stack and incorporated date. On the High Road front of this building, note the plaster decoration with a central panel sporting floral swags and the initials 'JWR', the brick pilaster effect with decorated tops and bases plus the swan neck, or scrolled pediments, above the first floor window. Adjoining at No. 294 can be seen a fine plaster panel decorated in swags and ribbons with a central shield with the date 1883. Below, the original multi paned sash windows, with their coloured glass, still remain. At Nos. 304 and 306 are two terracotta panels, one with the name 'Eagle House'. As with the rest of this architectural sequence, the chimney stacks are not left plain. Note the stylistic gables and the date 1893 on the last of the buildings before Ambleside Avenue. The building designs are attributed to Wheeler and Hollands, with the builder being the Hill Brothers, whose name and date can be seen elaborately presented in terracotta, beside the name panel 'Broadway'. Behind in Ambleside Avenue can be seen the Mews, albeit much altered.

Dyce Fountain

The Broadway

THE HIGH ROAD STREATHAM

96. THE TRIANGLE.

A sequence of quality architecture attributed to a local architect Frederick Wheeler and dated to 1885. The builders were Hill Brothers of Streatham. There is much to observe in this stretch of buildings which form a triangular development of shops and flats from Gleneagle Road to Station Approach. The main visual features are the gables. These are designed in the Dutch style, also seen in other nearby buildings. There is plenty of scroll type stonework enhancing these gables. Decorative plaster work and bold brick arches above some of the widows add interest to their otherwise plain design. Note also the low relief shaped brickwork panels. Horizontal bands of stonework unify the buildings. The focus of this development is the curved north corner, which gives the immediate area some architectural authority. The sweep of the curve is broken at ground level with the entrance to Triangle House. This has a scrolled pediment, brick fluted pilasters and some good decorative brickwork beneath the arch. Curving round the building, each side of the entrance, are distinctive windows set under slightly flattened half rounded arches with ornamental keystones. Note also the ornate name plaque below the central chimney stack, the patterned tiled roof and the attractive dormer windows with their angled shape. This well shaped building opened as bank premises. At the Station Approach end stood the ornate entrance to Streatham Town Hall, an entertainment venue, which was demolished in the late 1990s, nearly thirty years after the demolition of the Hall. The site is now Gleneagle Heights, which includes Churchill Lodge, a residential block which in design reflects some of the elements seen in the adjoining architecture, particularly the gables. Note the rounded tower feature with its cone roof.

97. STREATHAM STATION.

Before coming to Streatham Station is another modern construction, bereft of any praiseworthy design. This replaced Station Parade, a row of lock up Victorian shops. The present building is purely functional, with minimal decoration, and was, until recently, a supermarket. Sheet metal cladding, bare concrete pillars, green tubular hand trails and wire panels at the entrance add little to the buildings attraction. Inclued in the development, which dates to the late 1970s, was a lower level car park and the three retail shops seen today. The station, with its plain metal and glass frontage was built in 1991, replacing the entrance

The Triangle

Streatham Station

THE HIGH ROAD STREATHAM

Streatham Ice Arena

built by the London, Brighton and South Coast Railway Company. The original station, built in 1868, had its entrance in Station Approach and moved to its present position with the building of the High Road entrance in 1898. At platform level much of the original station remains. The present station with its 'economic' design and liken to a dark glass box, is a shadow of its predecessor.

98. 360-382 STREATHAM HIGH ROAD.

Next is a plainly presented brick building of two storeys with shops. Built in the late 1960s on the site of an unfinished pre-war building. Note the rather tall chimney stacks. Following stands a small narrow fronted building, a shop premises with a rendered façade and a stepped roofline. Part of the redevelopment of this short stretch of the High Road that was stopped by the second world war.

99. STREATHAM LEISURE CENTRE.

Visually a well proportioned and designed building with plenty of restrained brick and stone decoration. Opened as Streatham Baths in 1927. The design is the work of Ernest Elford, architect for Wandsworth Borough Council, who were responsible for the building until 1965. The main feature is the portico with its Tuscan columns and the above central bay built in plain stone, finished with an arched pediment. Other features to note are the raised blocks of brickwork, liken to quoins, on the corners of the two wings, the chimney stacks and the windows with their styled architraves, keystones and sills. Also, the decorative iron railings along the façade and the period styled entrance doors and glazing bars. The foyer area and pool keep much of their original design. Foundation stone to be seen right of the entrance.

Streatham Leisure Centre

100. STREATHAM ICE ARENA.

Unashamedly Art Deco in design. Designed by the cinema architect Robert Cromie the rink was formally opened in February 1931. The style is geometric relying on a symmetrical façade which imparts an Egyptian influence. Striking features are the tall recessed windows, which give simplicity to the frontage. Minimal decoration is used and is seen at the base of the flanking windows to the entrance frontage. This decoration is pure Art Deco and expressed in the manner of a

Discount Carpet shop at 382 Streatham High Road

stylistic vase of flowers. Note the use of patterned leaded lights in the windows, and also the end sections of the façade with their period door surrounds. The original signage and entrance canopy and foyer have gone, along with the decorative outside wall which was removed during the 1970s for road widening. During the second world war the rink was closed and used as a food store until 1946. Streatham Ice Rink was taken over by Mecca in 1962 and named the Silver Blades. Became one of the premier skating rinks in the country and, during the 1950s and 1960s, was used for national boxing tournaments.

THE HIGH ROAD STREATHAM

Streatham United Reform Church

101. STREATHAM UNITED REFORMED CHURCH.

A robust looking all-brick church built to the design of James Cubitt and opened in 1901. Grade II listed. Originally the Congregational Church. Designed in the traditional style of a medieval parish church. Accommodated 700 worshippers. Observe the chequer pattern of dressed flint and brick on the porch and transept, plus the carved heads and the wooden doors with their decorative hinges. Some interesting brickwork, including small decorative buttresses, course work, and that seen at the top of the tower. Here brick and stonework make a busy skyline. Interesting features are the buttresses of the tower which impart boldness and height. Note the window arches. Adjoining is the Church Hall, built in 1912, with some decorative features, such as the leaded windows, reflecting the Arts and Crafts style. Has a well proportioned frontage with black bricks giving some patterning and brick window arches of Tudor Style. Sadly, in recent years the building has fallen into decay.

END OF THE CONSERVATION AREA.

102. STREATHAM BUS GARAGE.

Not the most popular building along the High Road but nevertheless architecturally interesting to look at. This is

Streatham Bus Garage

basically a structure of yellow brick with red and yellow metal cladding and trimming, which gives some cohesion to the design. The building is block-like with the central area emphasised by two short towers. In between is a windowed façade with an overhanging roof, which adds interest to the frontage. Dark brick coursing above and below windows and along bottom edges give some decoration to the brickwork. View the side of the garage in Natal Road, where the architecture becomes more imaginative and colourful. Although aggressive looking, it was designed to be a functional building and was opened in 1987 to take 90 buses on six routes. Due to deregulation and the loss of bus routes, the garage closed in 1992. Today the main area of the building is used for Streatham Kart Racing and a few routes still use a part of the garage as a terminal point. The original bus garage was built in 1913 by the London General Omnibus Company.

103. CHIMES CORNER.

Adjacent to the bus garage is a large detached house of two floors dating to the late Victorian period. The frontage has been remodelled with a new facade, probably during the 1920s. Front rendered and lightly incised to give a stonework effect. Simple bay windows. A moulded cornice and pronounced quoins add some interest to an otherwise bare looking building. The name was taken from the Chimes, a large house which once stood opposite and known for its chiming clock. Following are two open sites, (cleared bomb sites from the second world war), divided by Lewin Road.

Chimes Corner

THE HIGH ROAD STREATHAM

Commonside Court

Hambley Mansions

104. COMMONSIDE COURT.
A little appreciated building dating to about 1934, built in the modernist style. The main features which stand out are protruding tower like-blocks with their iron rail balconies and the large central glazed stair well. Some decorative brick course work, notably above the first floor. Emphasis of design is on the vertical line. Note the thirties styled entrance. The chimney pots are modern (with mobile phone masts within).

Central section of 418-420 Streatham High Road

105. HAMBLEY MANSIONS.
Next, in a more decorative style, is a fine frontage of brick and tile. A visually warm looking building. Has a traditional English country style about it. The work of Streatham architect, Sir Ernest George and Peto. Built in 1877 by William Mason of Streatham Common. Originally designed as three separate buildings, they are visually unified by a pleasing mixture of traditional brick and tile decoration but have been spoilt by the addition of shop fronts. Although the brickwork is generally plain, the tile hung upper part below the gables is decorative. A squared bay with original sash windows breaks the flatness of the front elevation. Note the subtle tile canopies above the windows and the restrained use of red and cut brickwork. Above the entrance is a swan neck styled pediment. Some moulded brickwork and pargetting. View the side elevation in Barrow Road and the extended chimney stack with its decorative terracotta panel of sea creatures which imaginatively finishes the base.

106. BARROW ROAD TO GREYHOUND LANE.
The main building in this short section is a terrace made up of five sections of unified design (see picture on page 3). Built during the 1920s. The main feature is the central section with its arched dentilated cornice and below a stone panel with a most exaggerated keystone made of tile edges, which links the two windows. Note the chequered patterned arches, again using tile edges, above the windows on the first floor and their keystones. Also the raised brick design on the chimney stacks and the decorative use of stonework to separate the sections. No. 420a retains much of the original shop front. Next, No. 422 is one of a row of lock-up shops which turn into Greyhound Place. These date to the 1920s. Note the stepped parapet and the use of tiles to make a geometric panel on this property and on the one further along.

107. GREYHOUND PLACE
Following into Greyhound Place stands a late Victorian property, 157-159 Greyhound Lane. This has lost many of its original features and now looks somewhat bland. The dormer windows have been modified and now sit uncomfortably in the roof. The remaining stonework imparts an idea of the original design and decoration of the frontage. Most of the original chimney pots have survived.

42

THE HIGH ROAD STREATHAM

157-159 Greyhoud Lane

Greyhound Public House

108. GREYHOUND PUBLIC HOUSE.

An attractive building dating to 1930. Replaced a Victorian Public House which in turn replaced a much older building. Designed in the 'Tudoresque' style popular at the time. Plenty to look at with this building. Pointed gables with carved barge boards and other decorative uses of timber and ceramic tile. Note the chimney stacks and window styles. Also, the panel on the angled corner with 'Rebuilt 1930'. This date is repeated in the decorative rainwater heads. A guilded styled statue of a greyhound adorns the main entrance, which is well decorated with ceramic tile in mixed styles. This decoration extends around the ground floor to the small annexe on the left and to the side entrance on the right. The building has an old English appeal.

109. BANK PARADE.

This quality development, which extends from Greyhound Lane to Westwell Approach, was built in 1890 to the designs of Tooley and Sons. The main attraction of this long frontage is found in the stylistic use of brick and the bold gables, which show a Dutch influence. Unfortunately, these gables have been much modified over the years and bear little resemblance to their original design, save for those seen at the Greyhound Lane corner. Here they have retained more of their originality than further along. Note the heavy scroll features supporting the gables and their associated brick columns looking like pilasters. Also the incised brickwork patterns of foliage and shields below the arches on the first floor. Most appealing are the attractive uses of cut brick and the mix of red and yellow brick in the architectural design, which cumulatively give visual interest to this imposing development. The end section by Westwell Approach has been rebuilt in recent years. The entrance to the old bank, on the corner with Greyhound Lane, is flanked by square brick pillars with finial tops and a pediment feature above. Note the date above – 1890. Originally, there was a metal and glass canopy which ran the full length of the building, which was removed in 1939 (see picture on page 3).

Bank Parade, Streatham Common

THE HIGH ROAD STREATHAM

Silk Mill

110. IMMANUEL CHURCH.

This church, of which little remains except the tower, was built in 1865 in a free adaptation of 14th century Gothic ragstone. The architect was Benjamin Ferrey. Note the iron boot scrapers each side of the pointed arched entrance with its old red sandstone pillars and other Gothic style details. The main body of the church was demolished in 1987 to make way for the building of St. John's House, which, to say the least, stands lost in its architectural environment. It is visually and architecturally incongruous. However, this recent build does make some concession in its design to the adjacent tower. This is seen in its elongated recessed window space which dominates the frontage. Note the arched balcony and the decorative iron work at the top. The building adjoining the tower is the church hall, built in 1960, successfully blending with the tower with its ragstone frontage. The main features of the tower are the parapet of arches and the cupola. Observe the arched entrance and modern iron work. This church replaced an earlier one built in 1854.

Immanuel Church and hall with St. John's House on the right.

111. SAINSBURY'S FORMER STREATHAM SILK MILL.

One of London's important buildings. Site of the first industrial use of the Jacquard Loom in Britain. Built c1820. Grade II listed. Later, in 1838, the mill and site became a centre for the manufacturing of India-rubber goods. Became P.B. Cow in 1857 and continued so until 1986, when the site was cleared for a Sainsbury supermarket complex, which opened to shoppers in 1989. The supermarket offers little architectural attraction. Nevertheless the general look of the building, with it's pleasing elevations of brick and gently slopping tiled roofs, blends in well with the surrounds. Some decorative brickwork and dormer features with decorative tile work are to be seen. The green area of trees and shrubs by the entrance improves the ambience. To the rear in the car park area stands the three story silk mill. Being an industrial building, it lacks decoration save for a stucco band above the first floor. Above the slate roof is a clock tower, weather boarded with a dome finial and weathervane. Note the window arrangements for maximum light for weaving.

THE HIGH ROAD STREATHAM

112. THE BEEHIVE COFFEE HOUSE.

A grade II listed building and presently Henry Hughes and Hughes Solicitors. Built for the temperance movement in 1878. Designed by Sir Ernest George and Harold Peto in the Queen Ann revival style. Builder R & E Smith of Balham. Adjoins the supermarket from where the side and back elevation can be seen and appreciated. Note the effective use of cut and rubbed brickwork and highly decorative pargetting above the dormer windows, plus the decorative brick cornice below the parapet. To the rear, the hall is emphasised by five pretty dormer windows, noticeable by their arrangement and Jacobean styled pargetting. Note also the extended chimney stack on the side elevation which begins in a flurry of design, and also the nearby side door. This is graced with a fine decorative panel and a superb swan neck pediment above – the best of its type in Streatham. The frontage at ground level is dominated by the shop front with its white painted glazing bars and small panned windows. Above is a decorative wooden balustrade. Note the date 1878 above, displayed in large wrought iron numbers. In all one of Streatham's quality buildings.

113. PIED BULL PUBLIC HOUSE.

One of the old public houses of Streatham. Probably originating from the mid-17th century when Streatham Spa at the Rookery became fashionable. This building dates to the later part of the 18th century. Has a stuccoed classical frontage with the central feature being a large recessed arch with window. Note the fluted scroll brackets below the plain parapet and cornice. On the front of the building is a large coloured tile mural of a pied bull. This probably dates to c1920s, when the ground floor was modernised with the addition of ceramic tile decoration. Visual interest is given to the end entrance with its large pediment and other complimentary features, and with the striding row of arches with their keystones. Interesting metal work above door of a bull's head with leafy designs and lettering advertising Billiards. Note also the arched ceramic panels with the decorative ram feature. A remnant of old Streatham and coaching days.

508-510 Streatham High Road

114. 508-510 STREATHAM HIGH ROAD.

Nos. 508-510 are the only mid-Victorian house surviving along this stretch of the High Road. Yellow stock brick built. Most of the external features have remained making these houses of particular interest. The entrance to 510 is in Kempshott Road and is a feature of the side elevation, with its classical styled porch of Doric columns and dentilated styled cornice; a design which is repeated above the first floor. The five sided bay gives character to the front elevation of No. 508. Note the architrave surrounds and decorated sills and chimney stacks. A large section of the original garden wall still survives. No 508 was

The Pied Bull Public House and the Beehive Coffee Tavern

THE HIGH ROAD STREATHAM

544-552 Streatham High Road

the Streatham Modern School between 1908-1999 after which it was converted into flats with additions to the top and rear of the building.

115. 516-522 STREATHAM HIGH ROAD

This building complex fills the High Road frontage from Kempshott Road to Penistone Road, and is at present subject to redevelopment by Access Storage. The collection of buildings which fill the site originate from 1931 when it was redeveloped by South London Motors. The main block has that modernist look, popular with architects at the time. There are no architectural features of note. The factory buildings to the rear appear to be of the same period.

116. PENISTONE ROAD TO GUILDERSFIELD ROAD.

On the corner of Penistone Road is a single storey shopping development of the early 1930s. At present being developed with original frontage being retained. Nothing outstanding about this building but nevertheless typical of its period. Note the roofline and the corner with its pronounced cornice and square block styled pillars, also seen along the frontage. Adjoining, Nos. 532 to 552 is a parade of shops dating to about 1910. Plain in decoration with red brick courses framing the windows. Dormer windows and a dome feature above the last dormer window. Note the narrow frieze of decorative tiles above the first floor windows.

554-562 Streatham High Road

582 Streatham High Road

117. 554-562 STREATHAM HIGH ROAD,

This parade of shops projects more architectural interest than the previous. Red brick frontage with yellow brick side elevations. Noticeable features are the gables, with a serpentine shaped gable marking the centre of the parade. All the gables are capped with a small rounded pediment. Some decorative stonework above first floor windows linked by stone stringing. Note the rainwater heads and the decorative ridge tiles. Built 1904.

118. ARRAGON PARADE, 564-580 STREATHAM HIGH ROAD.

This stretch of commercial and residential properties to Glencairn Road dates to 1904. The obvious features of this parade are the flat topped gables and the window arrangements with their moulded arches and keystones above. Little other decoration to view. Note the date on the central gable and the 1930s styled shop front on the corner with Arragon Gardens.

119. 582 STREATHAM HIGH ROAD

A pleasing three-storey block of flats with an angled elevation to the High Road. Set behind a laid out green area. Has an attractive contemporary entrance area which links the two-angled block. Worth a closer look. Otherwise, little decoration to be seen except for boarding below the ground floor windows, vertical brick dividing columns and emphasis to some windows with raised architraves. Built during the early 1960s on the site of three house destroyed by aerial bombing in 1941.

120. 584-598 STREATHAM HIGH ROAD

This sequence of buildings presents a mixture of style and date. On the corner of Hepworth Road is a modern residential terrace, Nos. 588-598. It looks top heavy with a large gambrel styled roof, unlike the end block with its low pitched roof. Interesting entrances with vertical boarding and brick arch decoration. Built during the early 1980s.

121. 600-610 STREATHAM HIGH ROAD

Following are four detached mid-Victorian cottage type buildings. Unfortunately, three of these have lost their original character through modernisation. Note the dummy window and the original chimney stacks and pots on the last house, Nos. 608-610. Also, the brick arches above the recessed windows and door on the first house, No. 600. Originally part of South Streatham village.

122. MARQUEEN TOWERS

Next to these is Marqueen Towers, one of those buildings which is very much out of place. Built in the 1970s in the modern style, note the covered balconies on the top floors and the predominance of windows on the frontage.

Marqueen Towers and Nos 600-610 Streatham High Road

THE HIGH ROAD STREATHAM

St George's Villas, 656-666 Streatham High Road

123. 620-626 STREATHAM HIGH ROAD

Next is another modern box-like building of the 1970s, void of notable architectural decoration, being a shop premise with flats above. Built of yellow stock brick with some decorative boarding to enhance some window areas.

124. COLMER ROAD TO THE NORBURY BOUNDARY.

The row of properties to Nos. 628-638 date to the early 1870s and are a standard design seen in many suburban areas of London. Some decorative features around the windows, like the rough cast keystones, and cornice. No. 634 retains original shop front.

125. ST GEORGE'S VILLAS, 656-666 STREATHAM HIGH ROAD

Next is a garage, sited on a second world war bomb site. Following are a group of six houses dating to late 1870s, four of which retain their front gardens. Basic decoration using red brick courses and arches give unity to the group. Note the decorative brickwork above the modern tiled bays and between the gables.

126. 668 STREATHAM HIGH ROAD

Next is the former Sussex Tavern, presently The Feeding Tree restaurant opened in 2008. Built 1936 in a plain style with some limited brick decoration, notably below the parapet and the Tudor looking chimney stacks. The lower part of the building is rendered which adds to the general plainness of the building. Has seen some recent modifications to the roof. Closed as a public house in the late 1990s.

127. HERMITAGE BRIDGE

Lastly is Hermitage Bridge and the River Graveney which mark the boundary between Streatham and Norbury, Lambeth and Croydon, and the London – Surrey border until 1965.

Hermitage Bridge. Note the line of cobble stones to the left (south) of the bridge marking the boundary between the parishes and boroughs of Streatham and Croydon and London and Surrey.